INDIAN CRAFTS

Troll Associates

INDIAN CRAFTS

by Keith Brandt

Illustrated by George Guzzi

Troll Associates

Library of Congress Cataloging in Publication Data

Brandt, Keith, (date)
    Indian crafts.

    Summary: Explains how the North American Indians
used simple tools to make clothing, weapons, cooking implements, and ornaments from the raw materials around them.
    1. Indians of North America—Industries—Juvenile
literature. [1. Indians of North America—Industries.
2. Indian craft. 3. Handicraft] I. Guzzi, George, ill.
II. Title.
E98.15B7   1984   670   84-2588
ISBN 0-8167-0132-6 (lib. bdg.)
ISBN 0-8167-0133-4 (pbk.)

For thousands of years before European settlers arrived in America, the North American Indians relied completely on their own skills and on simple, primitive tools.

Nevertheless, they created beautiful, well-crafted objects. They made all their clothing, tools, weapons, cooking implements, and ornaments from the raw materials around them.

In the Eastern Woodlands, wood was the most available raw material. It was used by the Woodlands tribes in a great variety of ways. In the Midwest, buffalo hides were the most available raw material and were used by the Plains tribes in many ways. For the Indians of the West Coast, wood was plentiful, as were shells and other raw materials from the sea. And in the Southwest, clay, semiprecious stones, and grasses were among the raw materials used by that region's Indians.

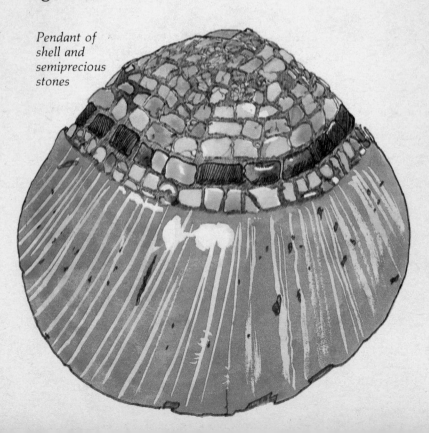

Pendant of shell and semiprecious stones

For the most part, Indian crafts were devoted to the making and decorating of useful objects. For example, baskets were used by tribes in all regions of North America. But no matter whether they were made from cattail reeds, from the rushes that grew in ponds, from yucca fibers, or from cornstalks, the workmanship was excellent and the weaves were pleasing to the eye.

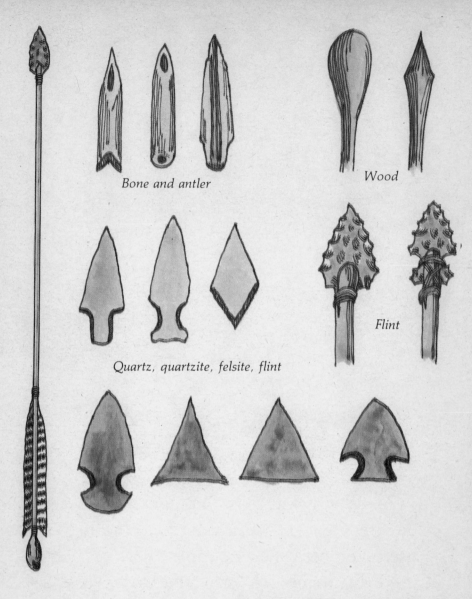

Bone and antler

Wood

Quartz, quartzite, felsite, flint

Flint

In the same way, considerable care was given to the making of arrows. Each tribe had its own recognizable design. And the Indians of different areas used different kinds of wood and stones.

In all cases, however, the arrow shafts were smooth and straight, and the feathers at the base of the shaft were trimmed and attached skillfully. A well-designed and well-made arrow was extremely important to the Indians who were hunters.

Not every article made by Indians was for practical, everyday purposes. The Pueblo Indians of the Southwest made attractive jewelry. The children of each tribe had dolls and toys. The tribes also had such sports equipment as hoops and lacrosse balls and sticks.

Eye-catching craftsmanship is also seen in the war bonnets, feather-trimmed peace pipes, masks, and other items made for religious and ceremonial use.

After trading began with the settlers, the Indians' designs did not change much, but the materials they used *did* change. At first, the Indians decorated their moccasins, clothing, and other articles with dried berries, bones, or shells. They also boiled porcupine quills in paint and used these softened, colored quills in their embroidery. Later, traders brought glass beads, threads, and a variety of manufactured items from Europe.

The Indians who lived in the eastern half of North America—sometimes called the Woodlands tribes—were especially clever in using wood and other tree products. Their main woodworking tool was an axe made of a stone head attached to a wooden handle. The axe was used for chopping down very small trees, splitting logs, removing bark in large segments, and for hollowing out canoes.

Using wood as the raw material and the stone axe as their tool, the Woodlands Indians built wigwams and dwellings, called long houses, of saplings and tree branches. They covered these structures with sheets of bark.

Bark was also used to make canoes, cooking pots, storage baskets, and buckets. And when the Indians tapped maple trees in the spring, they caught the sweet, flowing sap in long tubs made of birch bark.

Deer, moose, and rabbit hides were also important materials for the Woodlands Indians. The hides were cleaned with a scraping tool made from the shinbone of a deer. Then the hides were washed, soaked for days, and softened with a tool made of

an animal's horn attached to a wooden handle. This tool was called a beamer. After the hide was softened and ready for use, holes were punched along its edges. Finally, the hides were sewn together as clothing and footwear.

The Indians who lived in the warm Southeast did not need heavy clothing. The men wore a snakeskin belt with a fringe of mulberry bark in front and back. The women wore a short skirt of deerskin or Spanish moss. In cooler weather, they also dressed in a shirt of woven mulberry bark. For ceremonial occasions, the braves put on beaded moccasins, robes covered with bird feathers, and swan-feather bonnets.

The Indians of the Southeast crafted elaborate jewelry from shells, stones, feathers, beads, and metal. Conch shells were cut and smoothed to make hollow tubes. Braves used these tubes to hold their hair in a ponytail. They also used them as money. A hair-tube made of the right kind of shell was worth four deerskins.

Cane, another important raw material, grew abundantly in the Southeast. It was shaped into arrows and blowguns. The blowguns were used for hunting small land animals and birds. The arrows were used for hunting bigger game, such as deer.

Cane could also be sharpened into knives. Cane knives were only used as kitchen implements, because cane was not strong enough for heavy work. Heavy work, such as shaping a dugout log canoe, was done with stone axes and gouges.

The Plains Indians were nomadic, so they made only those things they could carry easily. They spent their lives following the buffalo, which was their chief raw material.

Buffalo roamed the Midwest in abundance and were used by the Plains Indians in many ways. Besides eating the buffalo meat, the Indians used the skins for clothing, footwear, teepees, and bedding.

The Plains Indians decorated their buffalo-hide teepees, clothing, and other articles with paintings and beadwork. The teepee paintings were different on the outside and the inside. The outside paintings were scenes of braves hunting on horseback or on foot, of animals and enemies being killed, and of tribal legends. The inside designs were geometric—stars, squares, triangles, and circles. The beadwork and painting on clothing and moccasins were also geometric.

Eagle feathers were used by the Plains tribes to decorate many objects. The number of feathers a brave wore on his head, and the way the feathers were cut or painted, told something about the wearer. For example, a feather marked with a painted dot meant the wearer had killed an enemy. A feather split at the end meant the wearer had suffered many wounds in battle.

Only the chiefs of the Plains Indians were allowed to wear war bonnets. The war bonnet was made of a buckskin cap to which a long stretch of hide was attached. The trailing ends of the hide were decorated with eagle feathers. The greatest chiefs of the Plains Indians also had buffalo horns attached to their bonnets.

Perhaps the most beautiful crafts were
turned out by the Indians of the Southwest.
Most of the tribes of this region were peace-
ful farmers and had a permanent, stable
society. These factors made it possible for
them to develop their craft skills to a high
degree.

The tribes of the Southwest used clay to build their sturdy adobe homes. Clay was also used for jars, pots, and bowls. These were shaped by hand and dried in the shade. Once dry, they were decorated with paints made from earth and minerals. Finally, the pottery was baked in a large, dome-shaped oven called a kiln. The result was a beautiful, long-lasting piece of pottery.

The Pueblo Indians usually put geometric designs on their pottery and on their finely woven baskets and blankets. But sometimes imaginative pictures of plants and animals were used instead.

The turquoise and silver jewelry, for which the Pueblo Indians were famous, was all made after the Spaniards came to the Southwest. The Spaniards taught the Indians how to use silver to make necklaces, bracelets, and other ornaments. Before then, Pueblo jewelry had been made of turquoise beads and bits of other colorful stones and shells strung together.

Tribes in the Northwestern region of North America were most famous for their elaborately carved and painted totems of wood. The totem, in the shape of a strange-looking animal, bird, or creature, was a kind of family crest. It identified that family, brought good luck, and kept away evil. Totems were used as headdresses, masks for religious ceremonies, and to decorate the poles that stood outside a family's lodge.

The Indians who lived along the coast depended on the fish and whales in the nearby Pacific for much of their food. They were highly skilled at making wooden canoes. They also made a wide variety of fish hooks out of bone and wood. In addition, they made large, basket-like salmon traps of wood, and other fishing gear of elk horn, bone, and shells.

After the settlers arrived and the Indians were herded onto reservations, the crafts of most tribes faded away. Indians came to depend more and more on machine-made goods. But fortunately, there has been a revival of interest in Indian crafts. Today, many tribes are working hard to keep alive the traditional skills of their ancestors.

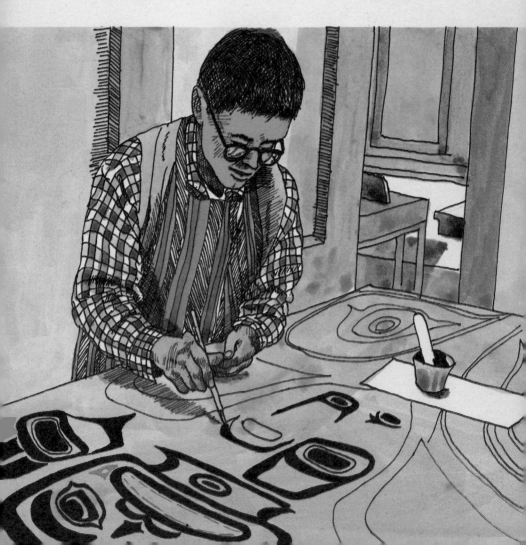